Art & Activities for Kids

Make Crafts!

Kim Solga

NORTH LIGHT BOOKS

Cincinnati, Ohio

97 96 95 94 93   5 4 3 2 1

Library of Congress Cataloging-in-Publication Data

Solga, Kim.
    Make crafts! / Kim Solga.
        p.   cm. — (Art & activities for kids)
    Summary: Text and suggested projects introduce young artists to basketry, weaving, leather tooling, and other crafts.
        ISBN 0-89134-493-4
        1. Handicraft—Juvenile literature. [1. Handicraft.] I. Title. II. Series.
TT160.S587   1993
745.5—dc20   92-44905
                                                                    CIP
                                                                     AC

Edited by Julie Wesling Whaley
Design Direction by Clare Finney
Art Direction by Kristi Kane Cullen
Photography by Pamela Monfort
Very special thanks to Theresa Brockman, Anita Drake, Libby Fellerhoff, Mark Garvey, Chris Keefe, Melissa Mitchell, Kathy Savage-Hubbard, Niki Smith and Suzanne Whitaker.

About This Book (A Note to Grown-Ups)

Make Crafts! features twenty-five unique craft projects plus numerous variations that will fire the imagination of boys and girls ages six to eleven. The projects are open-ended: Kids learn techniques they can use to produce handcrafts of their own design.

By inviting kids to adapt traditional folk art techniques, *Make Crafts!* encourages individual creativity. Children will create beautiful crafts that can be used and admired every day: colorful handwoven baskets, contemporary jewelry, frames, toys and games. Kids will get to work with fabric, rope, wood, clay, leather, papier-maché, metal, and other familiar craft materials. They'll get valuable experience in following directions, planning, creative problem solving, and seeing a project through to completion. They'll work on tactile skills such as weaving and pounding. They'll work on fine motor skills, too, such as gluing and stitching. And at the same time, they'll have an opportunity to express themselves creatively and produce something that will win them praise and boost their self-confidence.

A visit to your public library to look at books on folk art from around the world will inspire and delight young artists working with the same techniques.

Getting the Most Out of the Projects

While the projects provide clear step-by-step instructions and photographs, feel free to substitute and improvise. Some of the projects are easy to do in a short amount of time; others require more patience and even adult supervision. The symbols on page 6 will help you recognize the more challenging activities.

The list of materials at the beginning of each activity is for the featured project only. Suggested alternatives may require different supplies. Again, kids are encouraged to substitute and use whatever materials they have access to (and permission to use!). The projects offer flexibility to make it easy for you and your child to try as many activities as you wish.

A Note About Safety

The activities in this book were developed for the enjoyment of kids. We've taken every precaution to ensure their safety and success. Please follow the directions and note where an adult's help is required. In fact, feel free to work alongside your young artists as often as you can. They will appreciate help in reading and learning new techniques, and will love the chance to talk with you and show off their creations. Kids thrive on attention and praise, and craft adventures are the perfect setting for both.

Collecting Supplies

All of the projects can be done with household items or inexpensive, easy-to-find supplies (see page 7 for definitions of any craft materials you're not already familiar with). Here are some household items you'll want to make sure you have on hand: rope, thin wire, paper grocery bags, corrugated cardboard, paper plates, newspaper, scrap cloth, ribbons and yarn, wire coat hangers, old leather items, containers made of #6 recyclable plastic, aluminum foil and plastic sandwich bags.

Be a Good Artist

Work Habits

Get permission to work at your chosen workspace before you begin. Cover your workspace with newspapers or a vinyl tablecloth.

Wear a smock or big, old shirt to protect your clothes. Cut the long sleeves off of the shirt so you won't drag them through paint or glue.

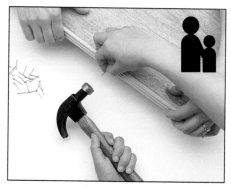

Follow the directions carefully for each project. When you see the adult and child symbol, have an adult help you.

Don't put art materials in your mouth. If you're working with a younger child, don't let her put art materials in her mouth, either.

The clock symbol means you must wait to let something dry before going on to the next step. It is important not to rush ahead.

Sweep up scraps and clean up splatters and spills as soon as they happen. Always finish by cleaning your workspace and all your tools.

How to Sew

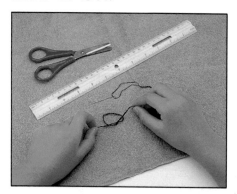

1 Cut a piece of thread about 24″ (61 cm) long and poke it through the eye of a needle. Pull the ends even and tie a knot.

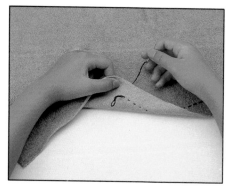

2 Sew with small stitches in and out of your fabric. Check each stitch to be sure your thread hasn't tangled underneath.

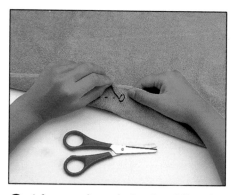

3 After you've stitched awhile, the thread will get short. Push the needle to the back of your work, make a knot, and cut the thread.

Craft Terms

Crafts. People create crafts when they make household things by hand. Craftspeople are very careful to make things sturdy as well as beautiful; this quality is known as "fine craftsmanship." Crafts can be colorful baskets, weather vanes shaped like fancy animals, lovely jewelry and handmade toys. There are many traditional crafts, with techniques and designs that have been handed down from crafter to crafter for many generations. In *Make Crafts!*, you'll work with wood, leather, rope, clay, and many other materials to make your own beautiful handcrafts.

Plaster of Paris. A powder you can buy at a hardware store or art supply store. You mix it with water to make a white plaster that dries hard.

Clay. A recipe for making sculpting dough is on page 18. You can also buy different kinds of clay at craft and art supply stores. Some dry in the open air, others require baking, and others stay soft enough so you can reuse them.

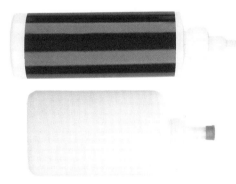

Glue. Most of the projects in this book can be done with regular white glue. For projects where you use cloth, *fabric glue* works better because it's specially made for cloth. *Carpenter's glue* from a hardware store works best on heavy materials like wood.

Ruler. Keep a ruler handy for measuring. This symbol, ", means inches—12" means 12 inches; cm means centimeter. There are about 2½ centimeters in 1 inch. This symbol, ', means feet; m means meter. There are about 3 feet in 1 meter.

Rope and cording. You can use many different kinds of rope and cord to make rope critters and yarn and coil baskets. Natural fiber rope made from hemp or cotton will work better than plastic and nylon ropes. Buy rope at a hardware store; buy cording at a fabric store.

Pliers/wire cutters. You'll need a strong tool called a pliers with a wire cutter to cut the wire when you make rope critters, wind fish and copper charms. A scissors is not strong enough. Ask an adult to help you work safely with any sharp tool.

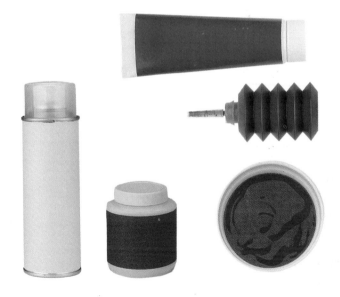

Paint. You can use tempera paint, acrylic paint, or fabric paint to decorate your crafts. *Tempera* paint (shown here in red) works well on paper and cardboard. *Acrylic* paint (shown here in blue) works well on wood, plastic, metal or clay. *Fabric* paint (shown here in purple) is best for cloth, because it won't wash out.

Acrylic gloss medium. Whenever you paint with tempera, and sometimes when you use acrylic, you'll want to protect your work with one or two coats of varnish. Acrylic varnish is safest to use because it's nontoxic. It comes in a spray can or in liquid form that you apply with a brush. Even though it's not toxic, it's advisable for adults to help you use any spray product.

Rope Critters

Fiber Art

It's easy to make creatures with rope, wire and string. And you can really play with them when you're done! The wire lets them stand up and bend any way you want them to. We'll show you how to make a horse. Start with three pieces of rope and three pieces of wire, each 15" (38 cm) long. Then use your imagination to create other rope animals and dolls.

Materials needed:

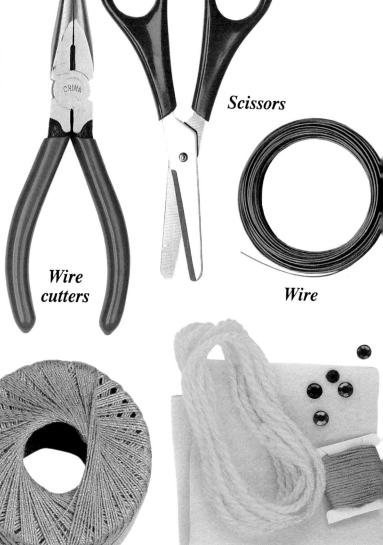

Wire cutters

Scissors

Wire

Rope ¼" (½ cm) thick

String

Decorations

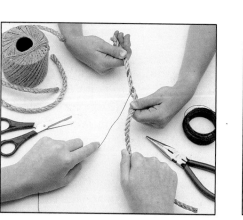

1 Twist wire into each piece of rope. Try to hide the wire inside the twists. It's easier if someone holds one end of the rope for you.

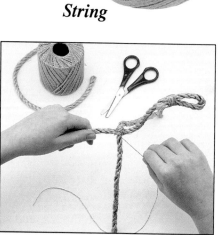

2 Make a loop and tie it tight with string. This is the horse's head. Tie the other two pieces of rope onto the body to make four legs.

3 Pull apart the fibers of the rope to make a fringe tail. Cut the wire out of the tail. Tie string tightly around the bottoms of the legs.

Glue short pieces of fringed rope to the neck to make a mane. If you want to, you can dress your rope horse with a ribbon halter and bright felt saddle blanket.

One long rope bent and wrapped with string creates this doll's head and neck. Another rope is tied on above the waist to make her arms. Then the rope is unraveled below the arms to make a fluffy skirt.

Use your imagination to make any animal you choose. Glue decorations onto the rope, or color the rope with felt-tip pens.

9

Weather Vanes

Papier-Maché

Weather vanes are made of wood or metal. They're flat so they can spin and show the direction of the wind. What weather vanes have you seen on the tops of old buildings? You can build a *replica*, or model, of a weather vane to decorate a room in your house.

Plaster of Paris, water and bowl

Materials needed:

Small box or milk carton

Scissors

Acrylic paint or colored markers

Black felt-tip pen or pencil

Craft knife

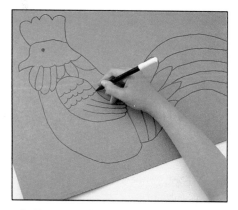

1 Draw a character for your weather vane on the cardboard. Make a traditional weather vane, like this rooster, or design your own.

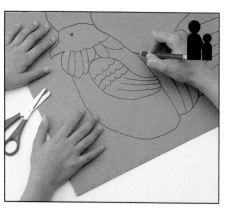

2 Cut your shape out of the cardboard. Use a strong scissors or ask an adult to help you cut with a sharp craft knife.

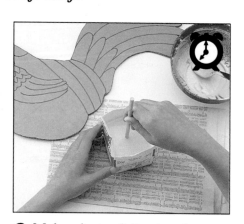

3 Make plaster following the directions on the box. Pour it into the carton. Stick the dowel in and wait for the plaster to harden.

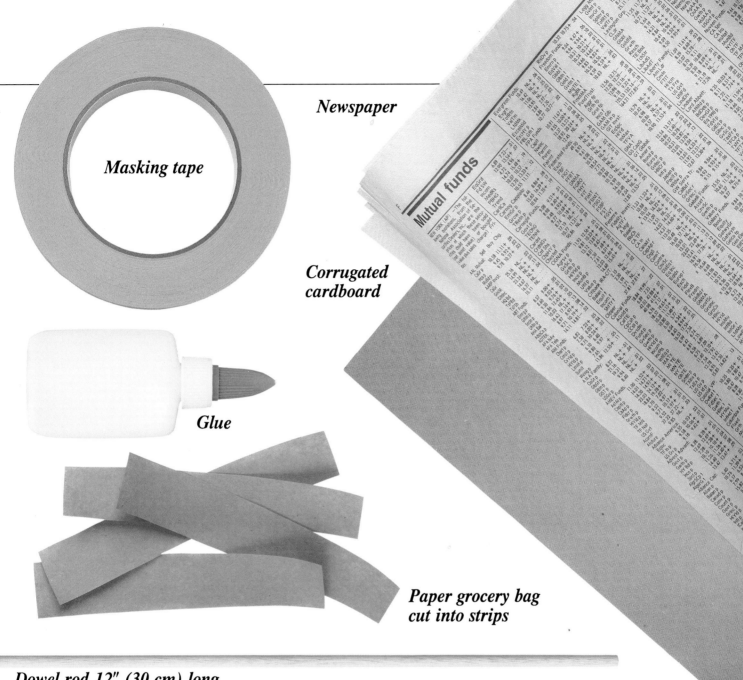

Masking tape

Newspaper

Corrugated cardboard

Glue

Paper grocery bag cut into strips

Dowel rod 12" (30 cm) long

4 Tear away the box from the hard plaster base. Tape the back of the weather vane character to the top of the dowel rod.

5 Cover all the parts of your weather vane with paper strips smeared with glue. Smooth them down. Let the glue dry overnight.

6 Paint your weather vane brown like wood or rusted metal. Let it dry. Add light colors with markers to make it look *antique*, or very old.

Weather Vanes

Here's the finished rooster weather vane.

This angel is painted black to look like wrought iron. Many weather vanes have arrows to point in the direction of the wind.

A horse is a traditional weather vane. But paint it like a zebra, and you've got an unusual work of art.

If you like building with papier-maché, try making different kinds of statues for your room or covered patio.

This whale looks like a weather vane made of copper. When copper gets old, it *tarnishes*, or turns green.

Yarn Baskets

Basketry

These soft baskets are just right for gathering eggs or holding small toys. They're so beautiful, no one will believe you made them yourself. But you can—with rope and colorful yarn or scrap cloth. Once you get the hang of it, you won't want to stop.

Scissors

Glue

Materials needed:

Fabric torn or cut into long strips, 1" (2½ cm) wide

Variegated yarn

About 5' (1½ m) of rope or cording

Big tapestry needle

Ruler

1 Tie a long piece of yarn to the end of the rope. Thread the needle on the end of the yarn. Start wrapping the yarn around the rope.

2 Wrap 2″ (5 cm) of rope. Bend it into a U. Poke the needle up through the end of the rope. Wrap yarn around the outside of the U.

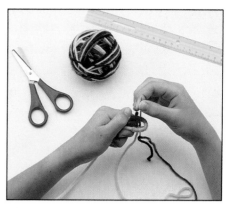

3 Wrap another 1″ (2½ cm) of rope. Curl it around the U to start a spiral. Poke the needle up through the center.

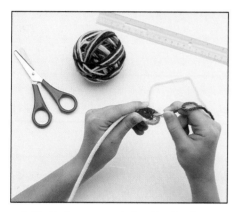

4 Pull the yarn tight. Push the needle down where the wrapped yarn ends, *in between* the two layers of rope.

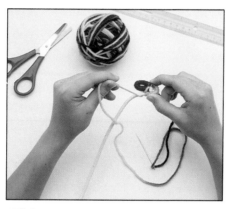

5 Come up around the outside to complete the stitch. You will make many of these stitches as you wrap and build your basket.

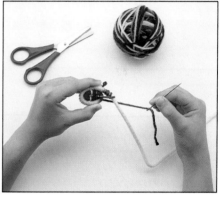

6 Keep wrapping. Every inch or so, make another stitch through the last row to pull the wrapped part in tight against the spiral.

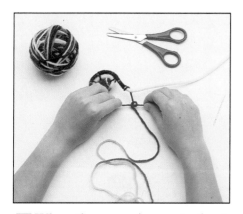

7 When the yarn piece gets short, take the needle off and tie a new piece of yarn onto the short piece. Thread the needle on the new end.

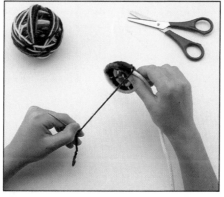

8 When your spiral is 3″ (8 cm) across, make the sides go up. Set the newly wrapped rope *on top* of the spiral, and stitch it tight.

9 When your basket is big enough, trim the end of the rope. Wrap the yarn as far as you can. Make a knot, and stitch it to the basket.

Coil Baskets

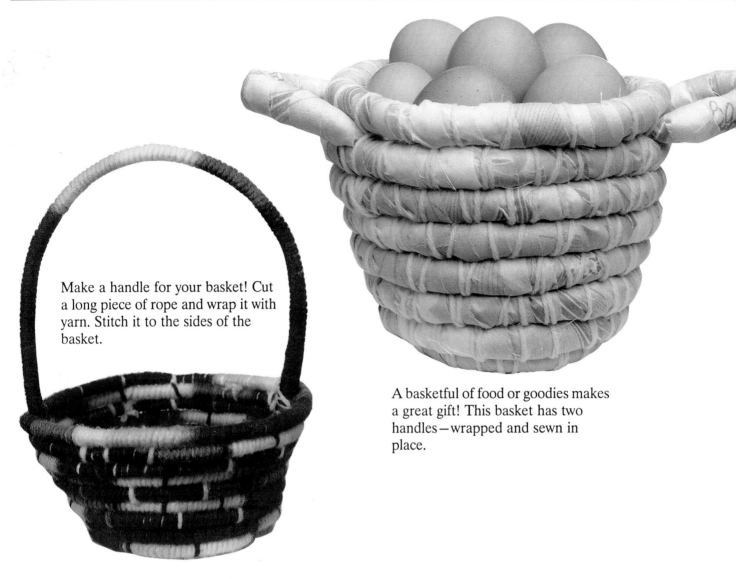

Make a handle for your basket! Cut a long piece of rope and wrap it with yarn. Stitch it to the sides of the basket.

A basketful of food or goodies makes a great gift! This basket has two handles—wrapped and sewn in place.

Rag Basket

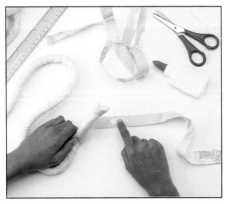

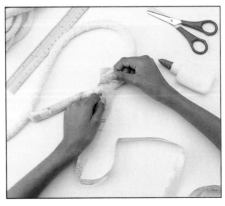

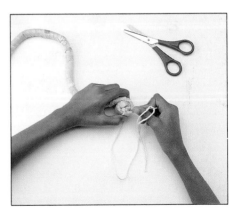

1 Cut cotton cloth into long, thin strips. Wrap these around a 5′ (1½ m) piece of rope. Spread glue on the strips as you wrap.

2 When you get to the last 2″ (5 cm) of a rag strip, place a new strip under it. Wrap them together, and then continue wrapping the new strip.

3 Keep adding strips until the whole rope is covered. Now coil the rope and use the stitch with yarn as shown in steps 2 to 5 on page 15 to make a basket.

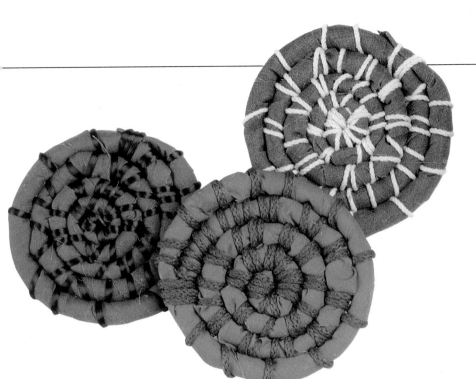

It's easy to make a set of coasters! Just keep building your flat spiral bigger and bigger, without any sides.

After you finish making your balloon basket and it's dry, you can add more glue where pieces of yarn and ribbon touch each other. Let the glue dry, and your basket will be even stronger.

Balloon Basket

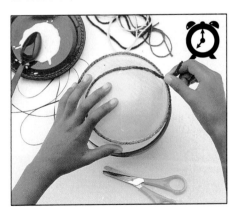

1 Dip pieces of yarn and ribbon in glue and wrap them around a blown-up balloon. Wrap in all different directions. Let the glue dry overnight.

2 After the glue has dried, pop the balloon and peel it away from the yarn pieces. Trim around the top of your basket.

3 Make a base: Cut a strip of heavy paper. Staple it to make a ring. Glue ribbon around it. Squeeze glue along the top edge and set the basket on top.

Jointed Puppets

Working With Clay

You'll love these silly dancing puppets! Make the puppets with either homemade sculpting dough or store-bought clay. Store-bought clay often has to be baked to get hard; follow the directions on the box.

For sculpting dough: Mix 1½ cups of white flour, 1½ cups salt, 1 tablespoon of oil and enough water to make a smooth, soft clay (about ½ cup). If the dough gets too sticky while you work with it, add a little more flour. Store in plastic in the refrigerator. It will dry hard if you leave it out overnight. Or, you can bake it in a low-temperature oven (250°F) for an hour or so.

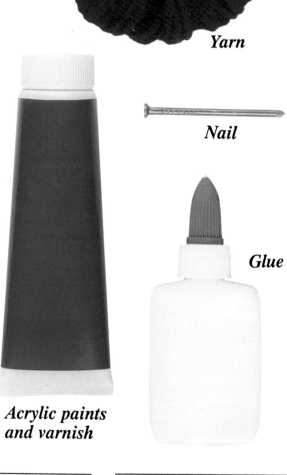

Yarn

Nail

Glue

Materials needed:

Food coloring or felt-tip pens

Acrylic paints and varnish

1 Shape a body and head out of dough. Pinch the shoulders out wide. Add bits of dough to make the face and clothes.

2 Use smaller chunks of dough to shape the arms and legs. Use toothpicks to carve details into each piece.

3 Poke a hole through the top of each arm and leg; shoulders and hips, too. Make each hole smooth and not too close to the edge.

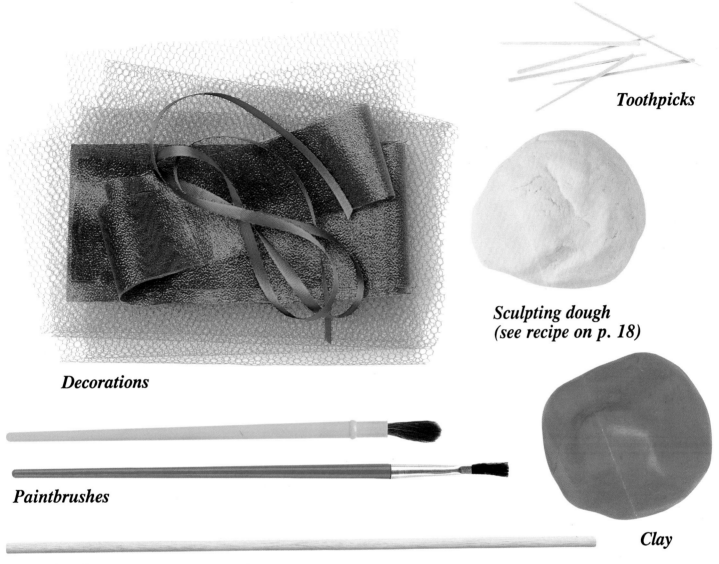

Toothpicks

**Sculpting dough
(see recipe on p. 18)**

Decorations

Paintbrushes

Clay

Dowel rod

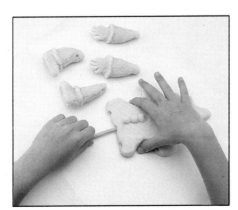

4 Hold the puppet with one hand and *gently* twist the dowel rod up into its back. Take the dowel out if you bake your puppet.

5 Bake or air-dry a dough puppet; bake a clay puppet. If you took the dowel out to bake it, glue it back in when the puppet is cool.

6 Paint your puppet and let it dry. Add a coat of clear acrylic varnish. Let the varnish dry, and tie the pieces together with yarn.

Clay Puppets

Princess. This princess is sitting on a dowel rod swing, and her legs dangle as she swings back and forth. To help her sit up straight, the pipe cleaner "ropes" are glued to her body.

Frog. This frog has extra pieces in his arms and legs. He moves not only at his shoulders and hips, but also at his elbows and knees!

20

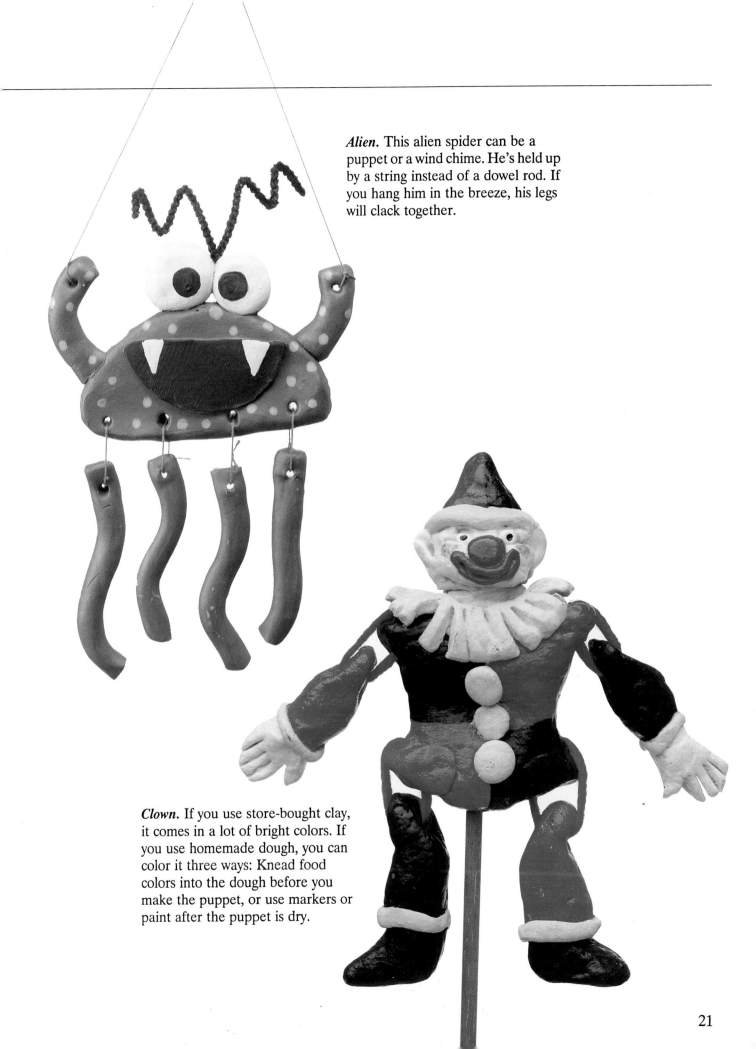

Alien. This alien spider can be a puppet or a wind chime. He's held up by a string instead of a dowel rod. If you hang him in the breeze, his legs will clack together.

Clown. If you use store-bought clay, it comes in a lot of bright colors. If you use homemade dough, you can color it three ways: Knead food colors into the dough before you make the puppet, or use markers or paint after the puppet is dry.

Frameworks

Sandpaper

Making Wooden Frames

A beautiful wooden frame you make yourself can turn any picture into a work of art. Save the sticks from frozen treats or buy a bag of craft sticks at a craft store. You can even collect twigs and use them to build your frame.

Materials needed:

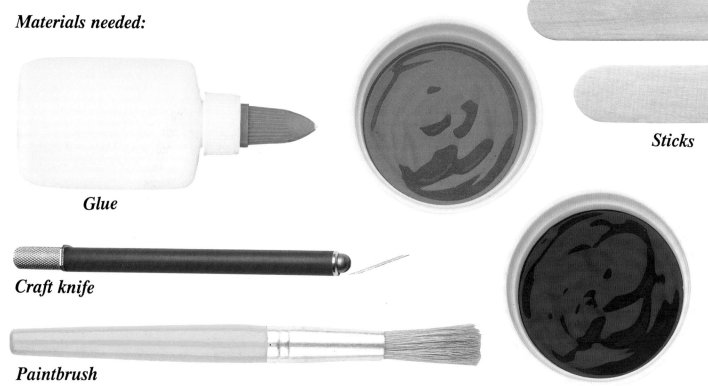

Glue

Sticks

Craft knife

Paintbrush

Paint

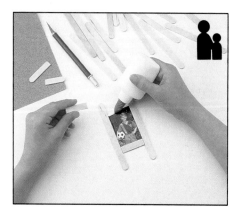

1 Glue sticks on the sides of your photo. Have an adult cut sticks to fit across the top and bottom. Sand the ends smooth, then glue them in place.

2 Glue sticks across the top and bottom, on top of the side sticks. They should overlap the first layer of sticks you cut.

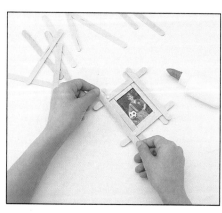

3 Glue two more sticks along the sides, then two more on the top and bottom. Keep building up and out until you get to the end of the sticks.

When you've built layers as far as you can go, let the glue dry overnight. Then decorate your frame with paint and little toys.

Build a frame with natural sticks! Have an adult help cut a lot of twigs the same size with a pruning clipper. Glue your photo onto cardboard. Then add sticks following steps 2 and 3. Use a lot of glue wherever the sticks touch each other. Be careful not to get glue on the photo.

Weaving

Weaving With Cloth and Paper

On the next six pages, you'll see how to weave a heart basket, a star ornament, and two kinds of place mats. You can use cloth or paper. It's fun to use colored paper, like wallpaper or wrapping paper. The best part about making woven creations is *using* them or giving them to a friend.

Scrap cloth

Materials needed:

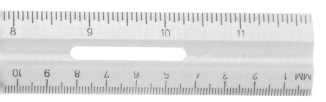

Ruler

Scissors

Tape

Pencils

Felt

Colored paper, wallpaper or wrapping paper

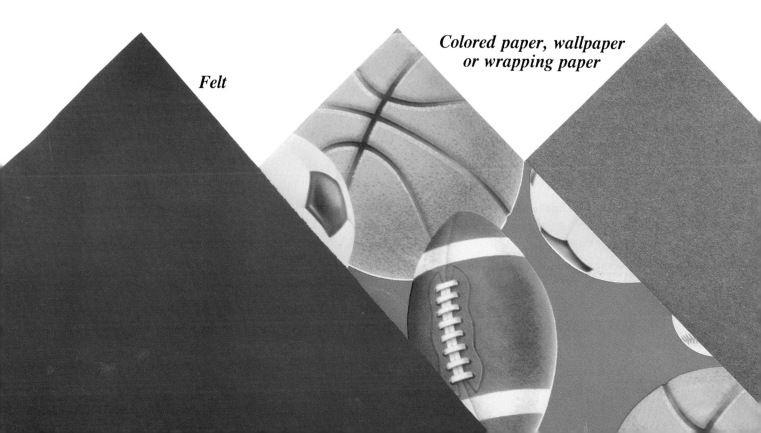

Clear, sticky shelf paper

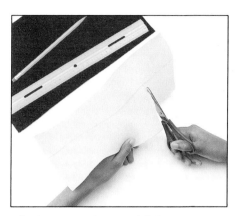

1 Cut two pieces of felt or paper 3″ by 9″ (8 cm by 24 cm). We show red and yellow felt here. Fold the pieces in half.

2 Trim the unfolded ends so they're round. Cut two slits in each piece, 3″ (8 cm) long, up from the folded end.

3 Now you're ready to start weaving. Slip a yellow strip _through_ a red one.

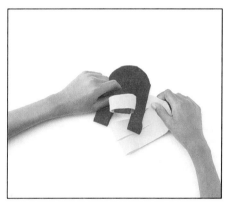

4 Push the middle red strip _through_ the yellow one. Then put the yellow strip _inside_ the last red one.

5 Do just the opposite for the second strip: red through yellow, then yellow through red, then red through yellow.

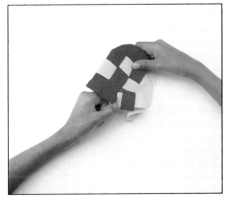

6 Now repeat steps 3 and 4 with the last yellow strip. Pull the felt gently, and you've made a heart shape!

Weaving Hearts and Stars

Turn your woven heart into a basket by gluing a strip of felt from front to back—on the inside—to make a handle.

It's easiest to learn how to make a star if you start with the same colors used in the steps on the next page. Once you get the hang of it, you can use any colors you want. Try using wrapping paper or colorful pages from magazines.

This heart basket is made of shiny paper. Cutting the strips different sizes really changes the way the finished weaving looks!

Cover strips of paper with sticky shelf paper that looks like wood to make a traditional ornament from *Scandanavia* (a region in Europe). Use a needle and thread to poke a small hole in the star, and make a loop of thread to hang it by.

1 Cut four strips of paper 1″ (2½ cm) wide and 22″ (56 cm) long. Tape two pieces together if you need to. Fold each strip in half, and cut the ends into points.

2 Place the red strip sideways. Fold the green strip over the red one, pointing down. Fold blue (or purple!) over green. Fold yellow over blue. Tuck yellow inside red.

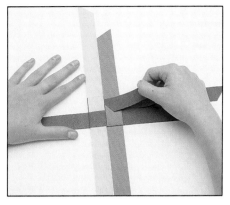

3 Push the strips together to make a square. Now fold one side of each strip back over the square in this order: yellow, blue, green, red. Weave red under yellow.

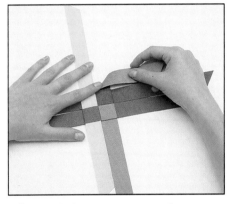

4 Bend the top green strip forward, then over to the side. Pinch the paper so it makes a triangle.

5 Twist the green strip around to the back, then down over the front. Weave it under the red strip in the square. Pull it snug, and squeeze it to make a point.

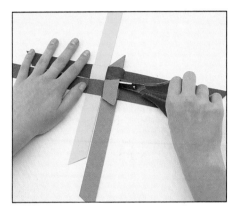

6 Trim the green strip so it's even with the bottom of the red strip it's tucked under.

7 Now repeat the action in steps 4 to 6 with the red strip at the left.

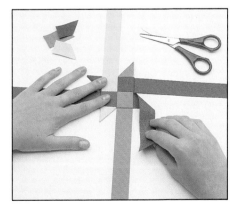

8 Now repeat steps 4 to 6 with the yellow strip at the bottom. Then do the blue strip at the right. Turn the star over.

9 Do steps 4 to 6 with each strip in this order: yellow, red, green, blue. When the blue strip is folded and trimmed, you're done!

Weaving Place Mats

Paper

1 Fold a big piece of construction paper in half. Cut slits in from the fold. Don't cut all the way to the end! Leave 1″ (2½ cm) uncut.

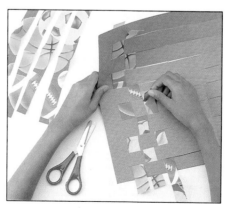

2 Cut 1″ (2½ cm) paper strips long enough to go from top to bottom of the construction paper. Weave the strips through the slits.

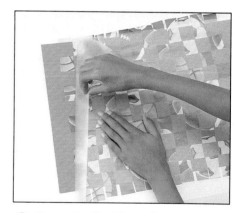

3 Cover both sides of the weaving with clear, sticky shelf paper. Smooth it down and trim the sides even.

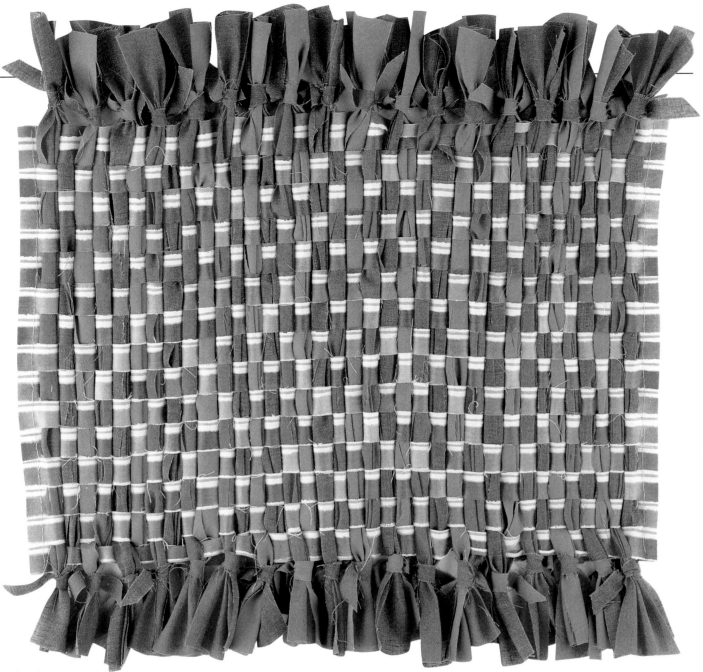

Cloth

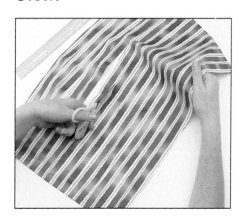

1 Cut a cloth 12″ (30 cm) by 18″ (46 cm) and sew around the edges. Cut slits from side to side. Leave ½″ (2 cm) uncut on each side.

2 Cut 30 strips of cloth 2″ (5 cm) wide and 16″ (40 cm) long. Weave these strips into the slits. Push them snug against each other.

3 Fix the strips so there are 2″ (5 cm) above and 2″ (5 cm) below the mat. Tie every two strips together with a smaller strip.

Wind Fish

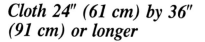
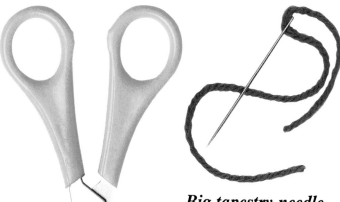

Building With Cloth

Every spring, Japanese children make wind fish to celebrate Children's Day. They hang the colorful cloth fish outdoors to flap and wiggle in the breeze. They look like fish swimming up a river. The traditional wind fish look like a kind of fish called *carp*, but you can make one that looks like a serpent or dragon or shark or any kind of fish you want. It's good luck to have a wind fish, and it's fun to make one of your own.

Cloth 24" (61 cm) by 36" (91 cm) or longer

Materials needed:

Glue or fabric glue

Scissors

Big tapestry needle

Pencil or felt-tip pen

Ruler

String

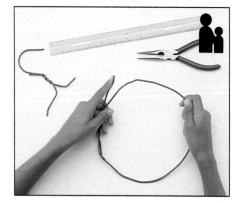

1 Have an adult help you cut an 18" (46 cm) length of wire and bend it into a circle with the pliers.

2 Fold your cloth in half lengthwise. Draw the side of a fish or serpent and cut it out. Cut both layers of cloth, but not the folded edge.

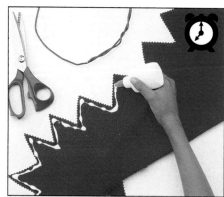

3 Spread glue along the inside of the cut edge, all the way up the side. Pinch the two layers together. Let the glue dry overnight.

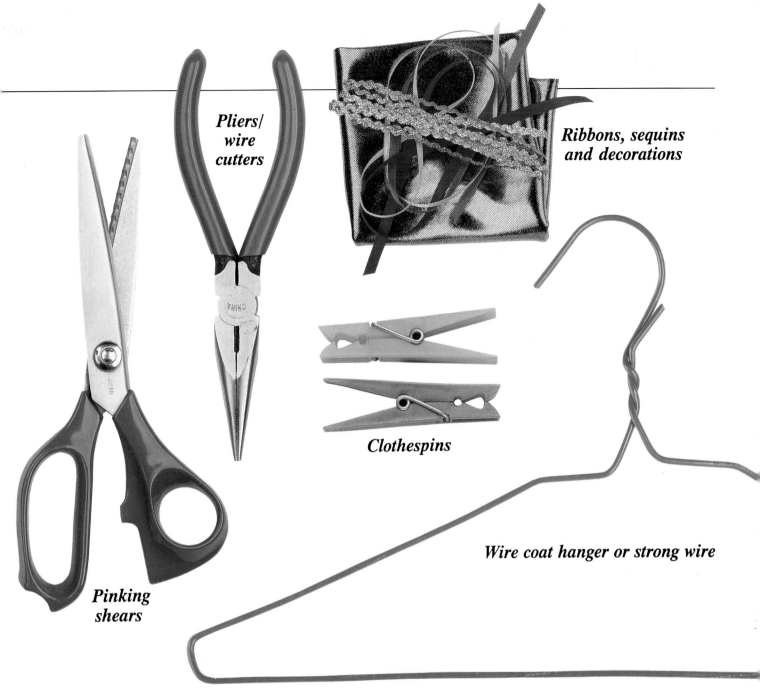

Pliers/wire cutters

Ribbons, sequins and decorations

Clothespins

Wire coat hanger or strong wire

Pinking shears

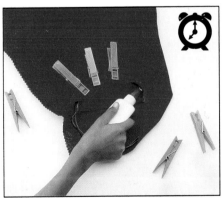

4 Put the wire circle in the opening at the top. Fold some cloth over the wire and glue it to the inside. Put clothespins on and let the glue dry.

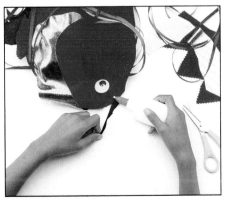

5 Paint your fish or add scraps of colorful cloth and ribbon. Use buttons for eyes. Add glitter, sequins, or whatever kinds of decorations you like.

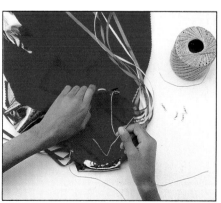

6 Cut three pieces of string, each 12″ (30 cm) long. Use the needle to poke each one through the cloth and tie it around the wire circle.

Wind Fish

Tie the loose ends of the string to one ring of a *barrel swivel* (shown in step 6 on page 31). You can buy a barrel swivel at a hardware store. It will keep the strings from getting tangled.

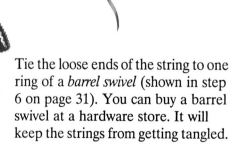

Here's a scary wind shark! He was painted and sprinkled with glitter while the paint was wet.

Making a paper wind sock is a breeze! Cut and staple a loop of sturdy paper. Attach long streamers of crepe paper. Add yarn as in step 6 on page 31.

Checkerboard

Woodworking

Checkers is an all-time favorite game, and it's twice as much fun when you play on a game board you make yourself! Buy the wood pieces at a hardware or lumber store. Ask if a clerk can cut the exact pieces you need. Or ask an adult to help you saw the wood. You'll need a 13″ by 20″ (33 cm by 51 cm) piece of plywood that's ¼″ to ½″ thick. And you'll need four pieces of ¾″ wide shelf edging, two that are 20″ (51 cm) long and two that are 13½″ (34 cm) long.

Materials needed:

Sandpaper

Hammer

Dishes for holding paints

Acrylic paints

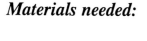

Ruler

Pencil

Paintbrushes

34

Newspaper

Plywood

*18 small
finishing nails*

Shelf edging

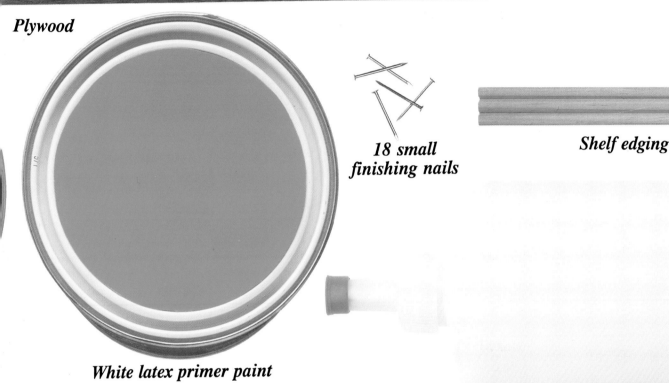

White latex primer paint

Carpenter's glue

Building the Checkerboard

1 Rub the cut edges of the wood pieces with sandpaper. Also rub the surface of the plywood that will be the top of your checkerboard.

2 Attach the long side strips to the plywood first, then the shorter ends. For each piece, squeeze glue along the edge of the plywood.

3 Have an adult set an edging strip into the glue and hold it while you nail it down. Use five nails on the long sides and four on the short ends.

Checkerboards

Paint colorful designs on each end of your checkerboard. Then have an adult help you add a final coat of varnish to protect your work. Make twenty-four checkers out of clay or sculpting dough (see recipe on page 18). Paint twelve a light color and twelve a dark color, and you're ready to play!

Painting the Checkerboard

4 After the glue has dried for an hour or more, paint the whole tray with white latex primer paint. Set it aside to dry overnight.

5 Draw a 12″ by 12″ (30 cm by 30 cm) *grid*. Make eight rows of eight squares that have 1½″ (4 cm) sides. Ask for help if you need it.

6 Paint over the grid with a light color mixed with a little water. The paint should be thin enough so you can see your lines through it.

You can make a cardboard game, too. Glue a piece of white poster board on top of a piece of corrugated cardboard. Color your design with markers or paint. Collect things to be the checkers. If you play with something that you can't stack, such as stones, paint a tiny crown on one side for the kings.

7 Paint *around* the grid and all the rest of the tray with a dark color. Let the paint dry.

8 Make a checkerboard pattern with dark squares like this. Follow the lines of your grid. Paint the squares as straight as you can.

9 When the paint is dry, you can fix any places that look uneven. Carefully paint over them with the color you need to cover the "goof."

Rag Bear

Doll-Making

This terrific teddy bear might become your best friend. Or maybe you'll make one of its rag doll pals. They're easy to put together with fabric glue and scraps of colorful cotton cloth.

Materials needed:

Fabric glue

Scissors

Iron

Crayons

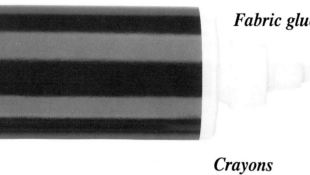

Sand

Coral

Dark Blue

Cinnamon

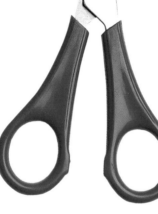

Clothespins

Cloth

Red embroidery floss, ribbon and buttons (optional)

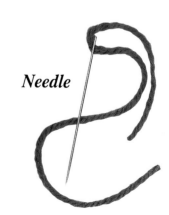

Needle

Foil and fiberfill (from a sewing store)

1 Draw a teddy bear on a piece of cloth. Draw a line about 1″ (2½ cm) outside of the bear. The space between the two lines is a free space.

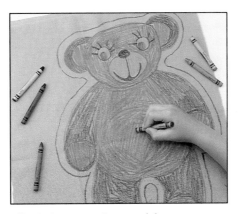

2 Color your bear with crayons. Color the whole thing or just the details. You can make it either real or silly. Don't color the free space.

3 Ask an adult to put your bear between pieces of newspaper and iron it. Cover the iron with foil before you turn it on; set it to medium heat.

4 When it's cool, you can stitch a red mouth and add button eyes and nose. Ask an adult to help if you don't know how to sew.

5 Put your bear drawing on top of another piece of cloth. Cut around the outside line of the free space so you have two bear shapes.

6 Spread fabric glue on the free space around your bear drawing. Leave 5″ (13 cm) with no glue. Put the plain bear on top and set a heavy book on it. Let it dry.

7 Carefully turn your bear right side out through the unglued opening. Stuff it with fiberfill.

8 Spread glue in the free space along the opening. Tuck the edges into the bear and squeeze it together. Put clothespins on and let the glue dry.

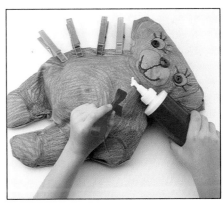

9 Make a ribbon bow and glue it to the bear's neck. Add any decorations you like. You can even cut out little clothes for it to wear.

Rag Pals

Here's how the finished teddy bear looks!

You can make any animal you want—just keep the outline simple. Make it with a colored cloth, or color it with crayons as shown on page 39.

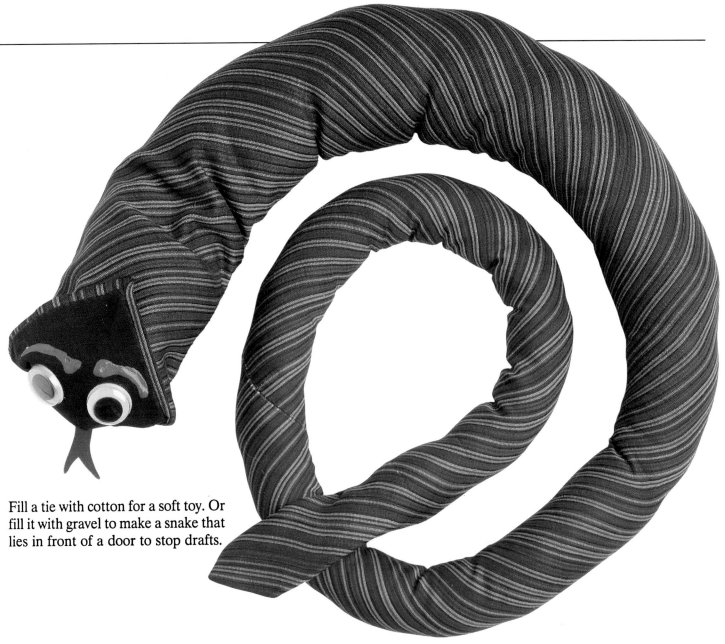

Fill a tie with cotton for a soft toy. Or fill it with gravel to make a snake that lies in front of a door to stop drafts.

Snake

1 Get permission to use an old necktie. Use fabric glue to seal the small end shut. Put a heavy book on top and let it dry overnight.

2 Stuff the necktie with cotton puffs or fiberfill from a fabric store. Use a stick or pencil to poke the stuffing way down to the end.

3 Glue the big end shut and let it dry. Then make a face with wiggly eyes, felt, fabric paint, and whatever decorations you have.

Beads

Jewelry-Making

Bright beads and crazy charms are fun to wear and simple to make. Everyone will want some of the beautiful jewelry you design! Never give your homemade jewelry to babies, though. The little pieces can be dangerous to them.

Acrylic paint and acrylic varnish

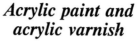

Cookie sheet and foil

Materials needed:

Toothpicks

Glue

Scissors

Nail

Elastic string

Paintbrush

Ruler (and pencil)

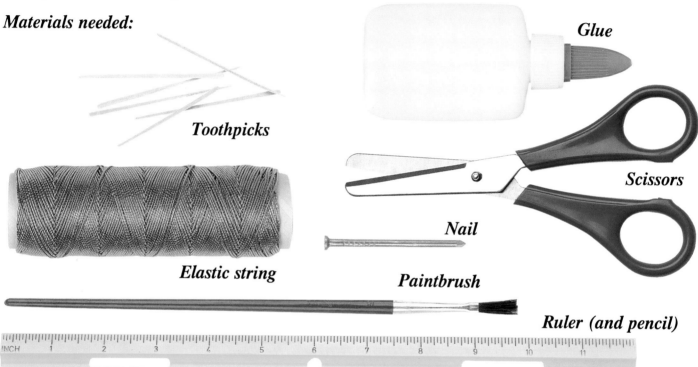

Paper Beads

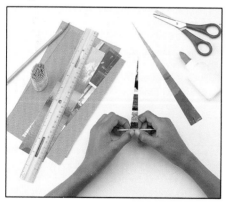

1 Cut paper into long, skinny triangles 1″ (2½ cm) wide at the bottom and 9″ (23 cm) long. Start at the wide end and roll the paper strip around a toothpick.

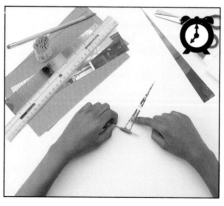

2 Spread glue on the tip. Finish rolling and press the point against the bead. Let it dry overnight, and then pull out the toothpick.

Wooden Beads

Buy wooden beads at a toy or craft store. Hold them on a nail and paint tiny designs with acrylic paints. Or color them with felt-tip pens.

Thin, colored paper

Air-drying sculpting dough (see recipe on page 18)

Wooden beads

Store-bought oven-bake clay

Clay Beads

1 Form beads out of sculpting dough or store-bought oven-bake clay. Try making balls, cubes, disks and pyramids.

2 Push a toothpick through each bead. Set the beads on foil on a cookie sheet. Let dough beads dry; have an adult help you bake beads made of clay.

3 After the beads are hard and cool, you can paint them. Have an adult help you add a coat of acrylic varnish when the paint is dry.

Beads and Charms

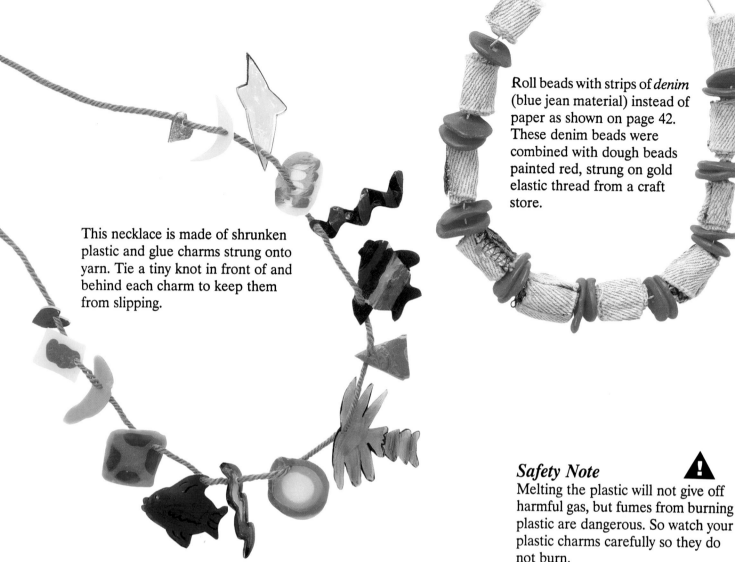

This necklace is made of shrunken plastic and glue charms strung onto yarn. Tie a tiny knot in front of and behind each charm to keep them from slipping.

Roll beads with strips of *denim* (blue jean material) instead of paper as shown on page 42. These denim beads were combined with dough beads painted red, strung on gold elastic thread from a craft store.

Safety Note ⚠️
Melting the plastic will not give off harmful gas, but fumes from burning plastic are dangerous. So watch your plastic charms carefully so they do not burn.

Plastic Charms

1 Cut big shapes out of shrinking plastic (from a craft store) or deli containers made out of #6 recyclable plastic.

2 Color one side of each charm with permanent markers. (Work outside or near open windows.) Punch a hole at the top. Set them on foil on a cookie sheet.

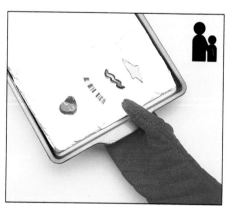

3 Have an adult help you bake the plastic in a warm oven (250°F) for three to five minutes. The charms shrink! Don't touch them until they're cool.

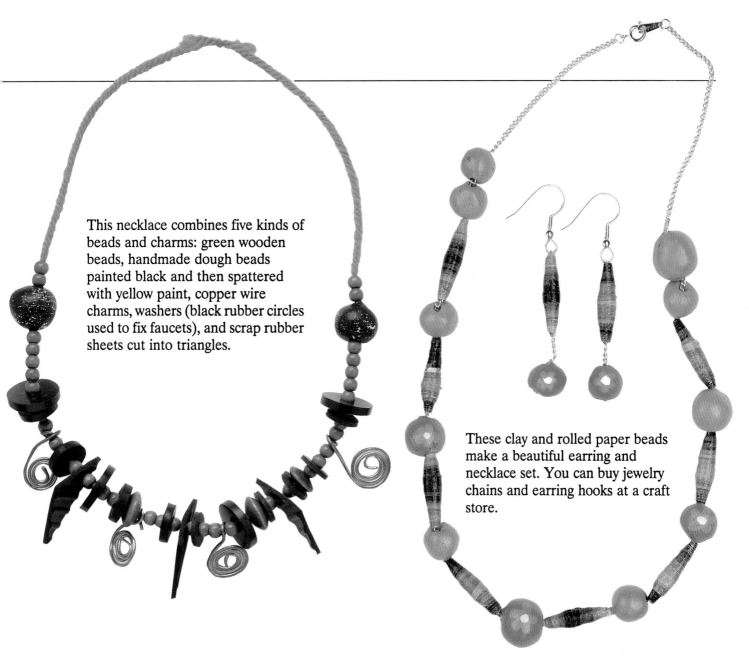

This necklace combines five kinds of beads and charms: green wooden beads, handmade dough beads painted black and then spattered with yellow paint, copper wire charms, washers (black rubber circles used to fix faucets), and scrap rubber sheets cut into triangles.

These clay and rolled paper beads make a beautiful earring and necklace set. You can buy jewelry chains and earring hooks at a craft store.

Glue Charms

1 Use store-bought colored glue or add a drop of food dye to white glue in a plastic bag. Snip a corner of the bag and squeeze the glue onto plastic wrap.

2 Let the glue charms dry overnight. Then peel them up and set them on a stack of newspaper. Pound holes into them with a small nail.

Wire Charms

Buy 20-gauge copper wire at a hardware store. Cut 4″ (10 cm) pieces with a pliers, and twist them into spirals. Bend a tiny loop at the top.

Leather Medallions

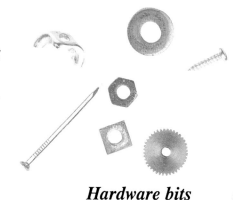

Towel

Tooled Leather

With a hammer, leather scraps and hardware pieces, you can make some great tooled leather *medallions* (small round or oval ornaments). Make one for a keychain, necklace, tree ornament or just for fun! If you have foil and an embroidery hoop, you can punch designs into metal, too (see page 48).

Hardware bits

Materials needed:

Hammer

Nail

Wood block

Scissors

Leather

Dish and water

1 Get permission to cut shapes out of old leather boots or purses; or use leather scraps from a shoe repair shop.

2 Wet a small towel and fold it on a dish. Slip your leather shapes between layers of wet towel and leave them overnight.

3 Set a damp leather piece on top of a stack of newspapers. Use a hammer and hardware bits to pound designs into the leather.

Here's a planet necklace.

An S-shaped ornament.

A star zipper pull.

A round keychain medallion.

4 Scrape lines into the leather with the tip of a nail. Always be careful when using any sharp tool!

5 Pound a hole into the leather: Place it on a block of scrap wood and hammer a big nail all the way through.

6 Let the leather dry completely. Then, if you wish, ask an adult to help you rub it with shoe polish. Or use acrylic paints.

Punched Metal

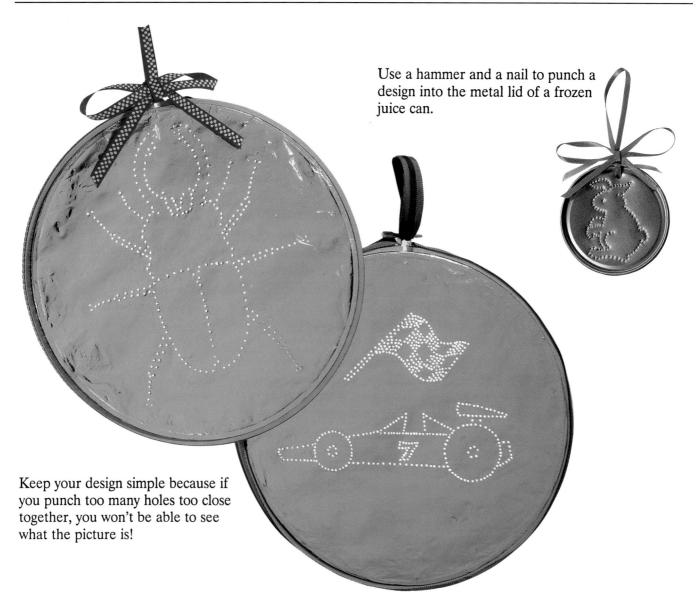

Use a hammer and a nail to punch a design into the metal lid of a frozen juice can.

Keep your design simple because if you punch too many holes too close together, you won't be able to see what the picture is!

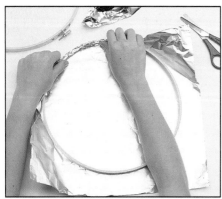

1 Tear off a piece of heavy-duty foil that is bigger than the embroidery hoop. Put the inside hoop on top of the foil and wrap it around the edges.

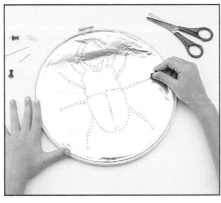

2 Put the outside hoop around the foil. Tighten the hoop. Use a small nail or push pin to gently punch holes in the foil.

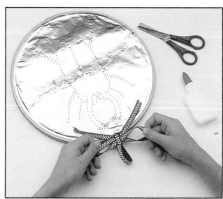

3 Glue a ribbon around the hoop and tie a big bow or make a loop. Hang the hoop from the top of the inside of a window frame.